EXPLORING THE
BISMARCK

First published in the United States by
Scholastic Inc., 555 Broadway
New York, N.Y. 10012

Reprinted 1994

Library of Congress Cataloging-in-Publication Data

Ballard, Robert D.
   Exploring the Bismarck: the real-life quest to find
Hitler's greatest battleship/by Robert D. Ballard.
   p. cm.
   Summary: Recreates the sea battle that sank the German
battleship Bismarck in World War II and recounts how the
shipwreck was discovered in 1989.
   ISBN 0-590-44269-4
   1. Bismarck (Battleship)–Juvenile literature.   2. World War,
1939–1945—Antiquities—Juvenile literature.   3. Underwater
archaeology—North Atlantic Ocean–Juvenile literature.
[1. Bismarck (Battleship)   2. Shipwrecks..   3. World War,
1939–1945—Antiquities.   4. Underwater archaeology.] I. Title.
D772.B5B3   1991   940.54'5943—dc20   90-15580   CIP AC

Design and Art Direction:
Gordon Sibley Design Inc.

Illustration:
Wesley Lowe, Ken Marschall,
Jack McMaster, Margo Stahl

Editorial:
Hugh M. Brewster, Nan Froman,
Mireille Majoor, Shelley Tanaka

Production:
Susan Barrable, Donna Chong

Typesetting:
On-line Graphics

Printer:
Tiber Officine Grafiche

Produced by
Madison Press Books
40 Madison Avenue
Toronto, Ontario
Canada M5R 2S1

Printed in Italy

EXPLORING THE
BISMARCK

by Robert D. Ballard
with Rick Archbold

A Scholastic / Madison Press Book

To my son Todd, who,
like so many young men aboard the *Bismarck* and
the *Hood*, died just as the glow of manhood
was beginning to burn bright.

Contents

Thousands of people crowd into the Hamburg shipyard on February 14, 1939, to celebrate the launching of Germany's biggest battleship. Cheers fill the air and onlookers give the Nazi salute as the ship is christened the *Bismarck*. Then the giant warship slowly slides into the water for the first time.

The underwater camera sled *Argo* moves slowly along the deck of the mighty battleship *Bismarck*. Three miles (five kilometres) below the surface of the Atlantic, the sunken warship sits proudly upright on the ocean floor. From their research vessel, Robert Ballard and his team can see the giant swastikas painted on her decks and the gaping holes made by British shells almost half a century before.

CHAPTER ONE

Search for the Bismarck

The Bay of Biscay, May 27, 1989

"How long have we got?" Todd asked. "What are our chances of finding the *Bismarck*?"

My twenty-year-old son Todd, and his two friends Billy Yunck and Kirk Gustafson sat with me in the control van on the deck of our research ship the *Star Hercules*. Soon this van would be the heart of our search for one of the most famous sunken wrecks from World War II.

"Twelve days on site, that's all," I replied. "I think our chances are fifty-fifty. If the ship is inside our target search area, we'll find it. If not, we haven't got a hope. Let's put it this way. Our chances are a lot better than the *Bismarck*'s were once the British forces cornered her and moved in for the kill."

The van fell silent. We all knew that forty-eight years ago today, British ships had shelled and torpedoed the feared German battleship, sending her to the bottom of the Atlantic. Now our ship steamed steadily across the same waters that had been the scene of this fierce battle as we headed toward the search area.

In a couple of days, Billy, Todd and Kirk would take turns guiding *Argo*, our underwater search robot

My son Todd *(top right)* and his friends Billy *(left)* and Kirk *(middle)* would pilot *Argo (below)*, our deep-sea camera sled.

with its video camera eyes, over the floor of the deep ocean. I wanted to be sure they knew the ropes.

"That video screen in front of you will show you what *Argo*'s video camera sees," I explained. "When the watch leader wants you to raise *Argo*, he'll give the command, 'Come up.' That means you pull back gently on the stick so that you don't increase the tension too much on *Argo*'s cable. If he says, 'Go down,' you push forward gently. Same idea.

"It's simple—as long as you stay awake. After seeing a million miles of mud you're going to find it hard to keep your mind on the job. It's a lot like driving a car at night on a straight empty highway. Easy to get hypnotized."

"Don't worry," said Todd. "Billy will have his U2 tape blasting in his ears. I don't know anybody

the Woods Hole Oceanographic Institution on Cape Cod, Massachusetts, had discovered the wreck of the *Titanic* in 1985. Since then we had been on many expeditions, each one pushing back the unexplored frontiers of the deep ocean.

But this was the first time I'd looked for anything like the *Bismarck*, once Germany's most powerful warship. Not only was she fast and sleek, her guns were the biggest ever mounted on a German battleship. When the *Bismarck* went on her first mission, the British were so afraid she would get out into the Atlantic and sink countless merchant ships that they

I look over the activity on board *(inset)* as the *Star Hercules* gets ready to leave port.

who could sleep through that!"

When the boys had gone, I sat down at the robot station and grasped the joystick control, which looks like it belongs to a computer game. I imagined piloting *Argo* over the wreck of the gigantic battleship that hadn't been seen for nearly half a century. It was in a room very much like this one that my team from

sent almost every big ship in their fleet after her.

Now we were about to relive that famous chase and sea battle, during which two great battleships were sunk and nearly four thousand young men died.

CHAPTER TWO

A Visit from Hitler

Occupied Poland, May 4, 1941

(Above) The battleship *Bismarck* is made ready for action.
(Facing page) Posters such as these encouraged young Germans to enlist in Hitler's navy.

"Psst…have you heard the news?" asked Alois Haberditz. "The Führer is coming on board!"

Heinz Jucknat rolled his eyes at his crewmates, Adi Eich and Franz Halke. Alois, their high-spirited friend, always had a joke up his sleeve.

"Sure," said Franz laughing. "Next you'll be telling us that the war's over!"

"It's true," insisted Alois. "He'll be here tomorrow!" Suddenly a loud crackling noise came from the ship's loudspeaker.

"Attention seamen of the *Bismarck*, this is your captain. We have just learned that the Führer plans to inspect our ship before we embark on our mission. We have less than twenty-four hours to prepare for him. Go to your battle stations immediately where you will receive further instructions."

Raising his eyebrows, Alois clicked his heels together smartly and gave the Nazi salute. "*Sieg Heil!*" he barked. The four young sailors quickly smothered their laughter as a commanding officer swept past them along the corridor.

"To your battle stations before I report you," he said sternly.

The alarm bells clanged and shouts of "Step lively! Step lively!" rang throughout the huge ship as more than one thousand men stormed to their posts. They ran, swung and sprang through the *Bismarck*'s maze of passages and compartments, sliding down companionways past sleeping quarters, kitchens, storerooms, common rooms, infirmaries and ammunition magazines.

The *Bismarck* was seventeen storeys from its lowest to its highest point. During their sea trials, Alois had explored almost the entire ship. When he climbed to the foretop—the observation post that was the highest point on board—it was like being at the top of a skyscraper. And the ship was a sixth of a mile long, the length of three soccer fields end to end. Its protective metal plating was so thick that it seemed impossible an enemy shell could penetrate it. Down in the boiler rooms deep inside the ship Alois felt as far from daylight as if he was snug in a bunker

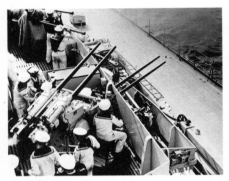

(Left) Antiaircraft gunners at their stations on the deck of the *Bismarck*.
(Bottom left) A cook sorts potatoes in one of the ship's galleys.
(Right) Loading enough supplies to feed over two thousand men.
(Facing page top) A cook ladles soup into pots which will be carried to eating areas.

① **Rudders and propellers**

② **Turret Dora (15-inch/38-centimetre guns)**

③ **Turret Caesar**

④ **Rear gunnery control station**

⑤ **Captain's and admiral's launches**

⑥ **Mainmast**

⑦ **Float plane**

⑧ **Funnel**

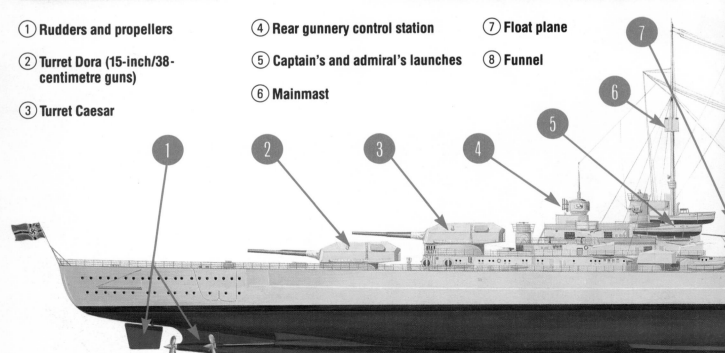

underground. The *Bismarck* was like a huge steel fortress, bristling with guns and teeming with people.

The four giant gun turrets each had two lethal 15-inch (38-centimetre) barrels that could fire at an enemy ship 22 miles (36 kilometres) away. The turrets were numbered A to D, from the one nearest the bow to the one nearest the stern, but everyone referred to them by name: Anton, Bruno, Caesar and Dora. Franz, Heinz and Adi served in the computer room for the two rear turrets, Caesar and Dora, while Alois was part of the crew who operated the smaller antiaircraft guns up on the deck.

Only a few minutes after the alarm bells had sounded, Franz, Heinz and Adi reached their

(Right) Painting camouflage on the ship.
(Below) Cobblers make and repair shoes in one of the workshops.

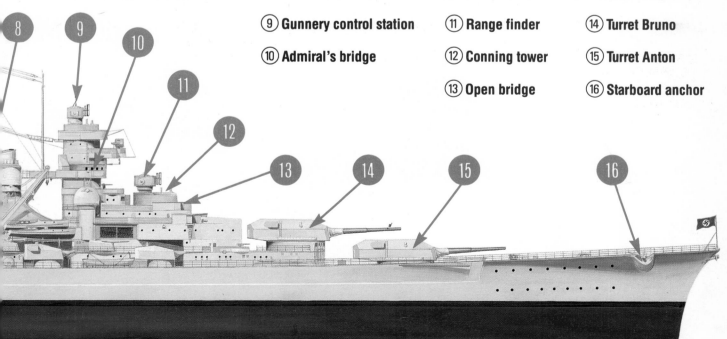

⑨ **Gunnery control station**

⑩ **Admiral's bridge**

⑪ **Range finder**

⑫ **Conning tower**

⑬ **Open bridge**

⑭ **Turret Bruno**

⑮ **Turret Anton**

⑯ **Starboard anchor**

stations. Here they had sat day after day during battle practice as heavy shells, each weighing as much as a small car, were lifted by mechanical hoists from the magazines situated below each turret, then rammed into place. Then, over the ship's telephone would come the order to fire. Franz, Heinz and Adi would listen through their earphones as the officer's voice fed them the information that would let them compute the variables needed to aim the guns with

maximum accuracy: "Enemy bearing one-four-zero, distance twelve thousand metres." The gun crews wore earplugs, but the sound was still deafening when the big guns boomed.

During battle practice the imaginary enemy battleship at which they fired the huge shells was always named after the famous British battle cruiser the *Hood*, the biggest ship in the British navy. Time and again the imaginary *Hood* was sunk. As the days

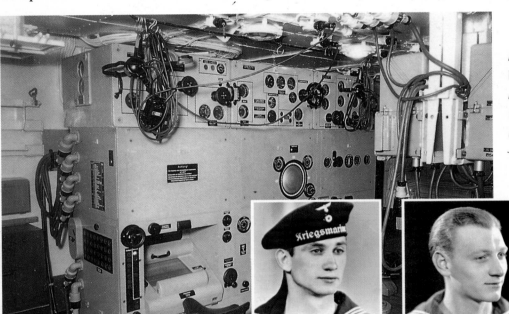

Adi Eich, Franz Halke and Heinz Jucknat *(from left to right)* **were stationed in the rear gunnery computer room** *(left)* **deep inside the ship.**

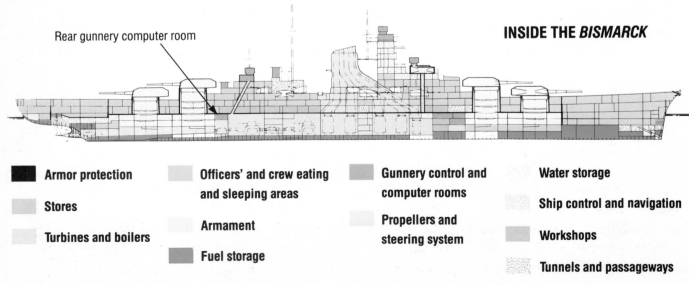

Rear gunnery computer room

INSIDE THE *BISMARCK*

- ■ **Armor protection**
- **Stores**
- **Turbines and boilers**
- **Officers' and crew eating and sleeping areas**
- **Armament**
- **Fuel storage**
- **Gunnery control and computer rooms**
- **Propellers and steering system**
- **Water storage**
- **Ship control and navigation**
- **Workshops**
- **Tunnels and passageways**

passed, and drill followed drill, the men on the *Bismarck* had come to hate that name with a passion.

Now, with the *Bismarck*'s first mission only days away, the men on the ship were thrown into a frenzy of activity with the news that Hitler was coming. The commanding officer in charge of the computer room briefed Adi, Heinz and Franz on the important visit.

"There's a good chance the Führer will want to see how the computer rooms operate. You will of course show him anything he wants to see as best you can," he instructed.

"Yes, sir," they replied, trying to imagine what it might be like to speak to Adolf Hitler.

Officers throughout the ship ordered the sailors to scrub decks, press uniforms and polish shoes. Even the ship's barbers had to work overtime to make sure every last man was presentable for the Führer's visit. Franz, who had trained as a barber before the war, helped handle the overload in the ship's barber shop. Heinz and Adi complained that he cut their hair too short, but there was nothing they could do about it. In one of the galleys, cooks hastily planned a special lunch for the Führer and his official party.

Alois Haberditz *(inset)* was part of the crew that operated the antiaircraft guns.

May 5, 1941

The day of Hitler's visit dawned clear but windy. The short trip from the wharf out to where the *Bismarck* lay at anchor did not agree with the Führer. He looked pale as he stepped on board accompanied by members of his staff. On deck the whole ship's company stood proudly at attention as the supreme leader of the Reich inspected the ranks. Alois stood stiffly as Hitler passed. Trying to stare straight ahead, he caught a glimpse of the Führer's gaze. Alois would remember that moment for the rest of his life. Hitler's eyes were cold; they looked right through him.

After the troop inspection, Hitler toured the ship. He seemed interested but said almost nothing. When he entered the rear computer room, Heinz, Franz and Adi were sitting at their posts. Their commanding officer described to Hitler how information such as the *Bismarck*'s speed, course, wind-direction and the relative position of the enemy ship was relayed to them from the gunnery control station high above. They fed this information into their machines and sent the calculations swiftly back to the gunnery officers in their control towers. These calculations helped the gunnery officers to correct their aim while firing the big guns in the heat of battle. At one point Hitler leaned forward to peer more closely at the direction-finding computer. He placed his left hand on Heinz's shoulder and his right hand on Adi's. Neither of them breathed. When the official party had left, the three friends joked about the experience, but they were also proud that their section had been singled out for such attention.

After four hours on board, Hitler and his party returned to shore. The thoughts of the ship's company now turned fully toward the mission they all knew was about to begin, although the exact date was still a secret. That night after supper, Heinz, Adi and Franz met Alois in the canteen where they talked of the day's events.

"I didn't like the look of the admiral. He looks mean," said Alois. Admiral Gunther Lütjens, who had accompanied Hitler during the inspection, would be in charge of their first foray into the Atlantic Ocean. His reputation as a cold commander was already making the rounds.

"I hear he and Captain Lindemann don't get along," added Heinz.

"But Lütjens was the one who sank all those British ships in the spring," replied Adi.

"I heard that the men who served under Lütjens all hated him," persisted Heinz. "Some of them are here on the *Bismarck*."

"I don't care if his mother hates him," Alois said, "as long as he knows what he's doing. The British have more ships than we do. They'd like nothing better than to sink the *Bismarck*."

At these words the four friends became quiet. Until now they had felt so safe on this vast, strong ship with its huge guns. But Alois had been to sea before. He knew what he was talking about.

The men of the *Bismarck* didn't know it, but the final preparations for their mission, code-named Exercise Rhine, were almost complete. Admiral Lütjens' orders were to link up with the brand-new battle cruiser *Prinz Eugen*, then steam as quickly as possible to the Norwegian Sea. From there, they would be in position to make a break for the Atlantic.

With Hitler's armies occupying most of Europe, Britain now stood alone against Nazi Germany, and she depended on convoys of ships that brought her precious supplies such as food, fuel and weapons from North America. Already German battleships and submarines had attacked and sunk some of these ships. If a battleship as powerful as the *Bismarck* could break out into the Atlantic and attack these convoys, the lifeline that kept Britain alive might be severed.

On his visit to the battleship *Bismarck*, German leader Adolf Hitler gives the Nazi salute *(left)* and inspects the sailors on board *(above)*.

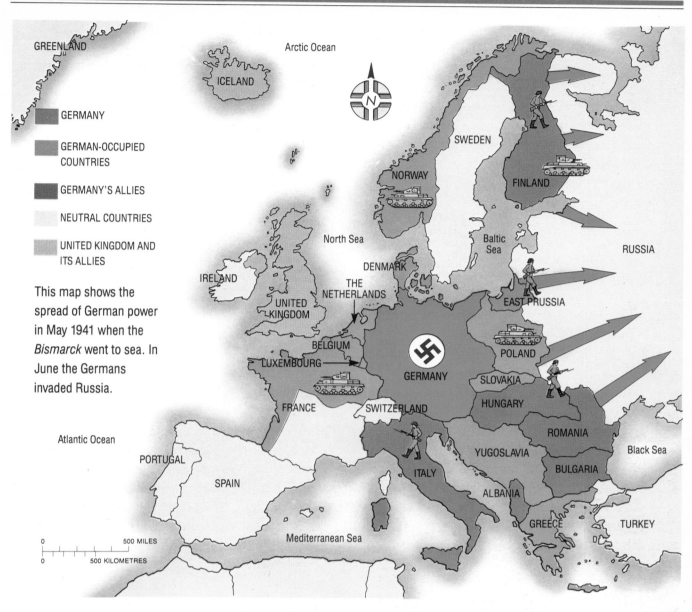

GREENLAND

Arctic Ocean

ICELAND

GERMANY

GERMAN-OCCUPIED
COUNTRIES

GERMANY'S ALLIES

NEUTRAL COUNTRIES

UNITED KINGDOM AND
ITS ALLIES

This map shows the
spread of German power
in May 1941 when the
Bismarck went to sea. In
June the Germans
invaded Russia.

SWEDEN

NORWAY

FINLAND

North Sea

Baltic
Sea

RUSSIA

DENMARK

IRELAND

THE
NETHERLANDS

EAST PRUSSIA

UNITED
KINGDOM

BELGIUM

POLAND

LUXEMBOURG

GERMANY

SLOVAKIA

FRANCE

SWITZERLAND

HUNGARY

Atlantic Ocean

ROMANIA

Black Sea

PORTUGAL

YUGOSLAVIA

SPAIN

ITALY

BULGARIA

ALBANIA

GREECE

TURKEY

Mediterranean Sea

0   500 MILES

0   500 KILOMETRES

The Second World War

In 1933 the Nazis took power in Germany, and the
country began to rearm. Six years later, Adolf
Hitler had reoccupied all the territory belonging to
Germany before its defeat in World War I and had
taken possession of Austria. Then, in September
1939, Germany attacked Poland, which fell within
a few days. Britain and France immediately
declared war on Germany, and the Second World
War had begun. Hitler's thirst for power and racist
beliefs brought suffering and death to millions
of people.

**Britain depended
on convoys of
ships bringing
food and other
precious supplies
from North
America. These
convoys sailed
together with an
escort ship on
each side *(inset)*.**

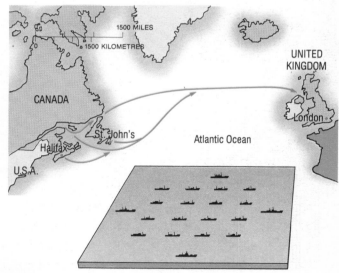

1500 MILES

1500 KILOMETRES

UNITED
KINGDOM

CANADA

St. John's

Atlantic Ocean

London

Halifax

U.S.A.

CHAPTER THREE

The Bismarck Breaks Out

Occupied Poland, May 19, 1941

"Adi. Adi. Wake up!" Franz's loud whisper was the only sound in the darkened sleeping quarters. First Adi and then the other men in nearby hammocks began to stir.

"What is it? Why are you bothering me in the middle of the night?" Adi muttered testily.

"The ship is moving!" replied Franz. "Our mission has begun."

By now someone had turned on a light and others were sitting up, rubbing their eyes and talking in hushed voices. Then the room fell silent as Captain Lindemann's voice blared over the loudspeaker.

"Seamen of the *Bismarck*. Exercise Rhine has now begun. Tomorrow morning we will join forces with the cruiser *Prinz Eugen*. Together we will sail through the Danish islands and into the Norwegian Sea. When the moment is right we will break out into the Atlantic Ocean where we and the *Prinz Eugen* will attack convoys carrying food, fuel and weapons to our enemy. I know you will all perform your duty with courage and honor during our difficult and important mission. Three cheers for the *Bismarck*."

Three *Sieg Heils* rang out in sleeping quarters and duty stations throughout the long ship as it slid westward through the starless night. Adi, Franz and Heinz talked for awhile, then tried to get back to sleep. But this proved difficult now that the months

This photograph taken from the deck of *Prinz Eugen* shows the *Bismarck* in the Norwegian fjords.

of waiting were finally over.

Far above, on the bridge, Captain Lindemann was also wide awake. Unlike most of the sailors on the *Bismarck*, he was aware of the elaborate and careful planning that had gone into Exercise Rhine. He also knew how difficult and daring their mission was. There were only two routes into the Atlantic, but both passages were constantly patrolled by British ships and planes. Breaking through either of them would require absolute secrecy, perfect timing, great skill and luck.

The Fjords near Bergen, Norway, *May 21, 1941*

Two days later, the *Bismarck* and *Prinz Eugen* entered the protected fjords near Bergen, Norway. They had already come a long way and, as far as they knew, no enemy eyes had spotted them. The stop was not scheduled, but Admiral Lütjens had decided to take the opportunity to refuel *Prinz Eugen*, which had smaller fuel tanks than the *Bismarck*. While refueling was taking place, crews painted out the black and white camouflage markings on the side of her hull with dull gray so that the ships would blend into the misty North Atlantic seascape. After leaving the fjords, the giant swastikas on the bow and stern decks would also be painted over. Their purpose was to identify the ships to friendly aircraft—but soon they would be far out of range of German fliers.

It was a beautiful sunny afternoon, and many of the sailors were permitted to go up on deck to get some exercise. Heinz, Adi and Franz admired the steep, tree-clad slopes of the fjords and noted that some of the peaks still had snow on them. This was the farthest any of them had ever been from home. At one point,

Lieutenant-Commander Müllenheim-Rechberg.

they spotted one of the *Bismarck*'s gunnery officers, Lieutenant-Commander Burkard Baron von Müllenheim-Rechberg, leaning over the railing staring at the refueling operations. In a few hours the ship was under way again.

It was almost midnight when Müllenheim-Rechberg took a last walk on the *Bismarck*'s deck before heading to his cabin. As he watched the distant Norwegian coast fade from view, he couldn't shake off the feeling of worry that he'd experienced earlier in the day when he'd watched the *Prinz Eugen* being refueled while the *Bismarck* had sat idly by. Why had Admiral Lütjens failed to refuel the *Bismarck*? Müllenheim-Rechberg had served under Lütjens before and knew him to be a resourceful commander. Was the admiral, perhaps, losing his touch?

Suddenly Müllenheim-Rechberg noticed yellow, white and red lights flickering over the coast. If he had known what they meant he would have been even more worried. This was antiaircraft fire provoked by British bombers sent to attack the ships. The Germans didn't know it, but they had been spotted earlier that day by a high-flying British Spitfire reconnaissance plane.

The enemy was already on their trail.

A British Spitfire spots the German ships in the fjords.

The Denmark Strait,
May 22, 1941

It seemed to Franz, Heinz and Adi that they had been in the computer room for days. They were supposed to be on high alert because the *Bismarck* and *Prinz Eugen* were now approaching the Denmark Strait, the passage that Admiral Lütjens had chosen for his attempted breakout into the Atlantic. But with no sign of enemy ships there was nothing for the men to do except try to stay awake by playing cards and telling

The route of the *Bismarck* and *Prinz Eugen* from the Baltic Sea to the Denmark Strait.

jokes. Fortunately, Heinz seemed to have an endless supply of these, though their commanding officer obviously disapproved. "This is a war, not a picnic," he had said.

"Attention! attention! Enemy cruiser sighted bearing green one-five-zero." At these words over the loudspeaker everyone suddenly sat up straight.

"Ach," muttered their commander. "I fear the British have found us."

The North Atlantic Ocean,
May 24, 1941

Admiral Lütjens had dozed fitfully through the pale half-light of the Arctic night. He was troubled. Last night his attempt to sneak into the Atlantic undetected had failed. And since then, he had been unable to shake off two British cruisers that were tracking them. In addition, the enemy seemed to possess a new radar system far more powerful than anything the Germans had developed. What other surprises did the British have in store?

Lütjens looked at his watch as his crewman brought him his morning coffee. It was 5 a.m. If only he could give his pursuers the slip before the cruisers were joined by other warships.

"Sir, a message from Captain Lindemann," said the crewman, handing Lütjens a note.

The admiral took the piece of paper and read it without twitching a muscle, but inwardly he groaned. The *Prinz Eugen*'s hydrophones had just picked up the sound of high-speed propellers. If these were British battleships, where had they come from? His last intelligence report from Berlin assured him the British fleet was still hundreds of miles away.

Suddenly the alarm bells began to ring, calling the men to their battle stations. Lütjens quickly buttoned up his uniform and headed for the battleship's bridge one deck below.

A few moments later he was standing beside Captain Lindemann, intently watching the southern horizon. Dark smudges of smoke soon appeared—a sure sign of big ships making top speed. Then mast tips came into view and began to grow rapidly into the unmistakable forms of warships.

"I don't like the look of those at all," began Lindemann. "They're battleships, if I'm not mistaken." But he could not hide the excitement he felt at the prospect of the *Bismarck*'s first fight.

"Let us hope you are wrong, Captain," Lütjens replied coolly. "As you well know, our orders are to avoid a sea battle."

Down at their posts in the computer room, Franz, Heinz and Adi could hear the conversations of the gunnery officers through their headphones. They

listened with half an ear while they feverishly computed the variables that determined the gunners' aim.

"Lead ship has fired its first salvo," the first gunnery officer announced matter-of-factly, and then there was silence.

Why didn't the *Bismarck* respond, the three friends wondered. Was Admiral Lütjens hoping to outrun the British ships?

"The *Hood*—it's the *Hood*!" they heard the second gunnery officer shout. This was the name most feared by every man on board the *Bismarck*. The *Hood*, their imaginary enemy during battle practice, was the biggest ship in the whole Royal Navy. A first salvo from the enemy would soon have covered the 13-mile

Launched just after the First World War, the *Hood* was the most famous battle cruiser in the British Royal Navy. The British depended on the *Hood* to defend them at sea.

(21-kilometre) distance between them, but still Admiral Lütjens hesitated.

Finally, with tension among the officers and crews about to explode, Lütjens' order came.

"Permission to fire!"

Even from deep within the ship, Franz, Heinz and Adi could hear and feel that first salvo when the *Bismarck*'s eight 15-inch (38-centimetre) guns fired in close succession. There was a distant rumble and an accompanying vibration, like an earthquake.

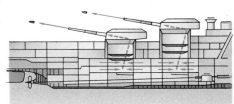

Heavy shells were hoisted from deep inside the ship to the gun turrets *(right)* and then fired *(left)*.

"Short," muttered the first gunnery officer. Adjusting the angle and bearing of the guns, he ordered another salvo. "Long."

For those on the bridge, in the gunnery control stations, or worst of all in the turrets themselves, each salvo was a bone-rattling, mind-numbing experience—like being next to a bomb going off. The roar was deafening, the sudden increase in air pressure made it almost impossible to breathe, and the thick brown smoke choked and blinded them. By the time the smoke

began to clear, more shells had been loaded and the great guns roared again.

Up on deck, Alois had a ringside seat for the battle. Since there were no enemy planes, there was nothing for him and the rest of the antiaircraft crew to do but watch and pray. The two enemy ships closed in rapidly. It was bright and sunny, so everything stood out clearly.

As the *Hood* sinks beneath billowing smoke and flames, the *Prince of Wales* swerves to avoid the wreckage.

Alois saw the puffs of smoke when the British opened fire, then waited twenty seconds and saw the shells land harmlessly near the *Prinz Eugen*, which was in the lead. It was almost unreal, he thought. You couldn't see the faces of your enemy or hear their guns. It was just one grim war machine against another.

Nonetheless, what he saw next would stay with him for the rest of his life. The two sets of ships continued to exchange fire. Then Alois saw a burst of flame on the *Hood*, the lead British ship.

"A hit!" he shouted, and everyone in his crew cheered. He could see that the enemy vessels were now turning slightly away from them so that their rear turrets would be able to fire as well. But suddenly something was very wrong with the *Hood*. A huge flame shot into the air followed by a great pillar of smoke. Then the warship split into two—its bow and stern both pointing into the air before it swiftly and soundlessly disappeared beneath the waves. In a matter of seconds nothing remained of the mighty *Hood* but a pall of black smoke.

It happened so fast that Alois was too stunned to speak. Then suddenly the antiaircraft crew started cheering wildly. Slowly Alois joined them, as they jumped up and down throwing their caps into the air. But inside he felt hollow. He couldn't help thinking about the hundreds of sailors who must have been killed instantly inside the British ship.

The remaining enemy battleship bravely continued

This photograph of the ship's company aboard the *Hood* was taken in 1939. When the *Hood* went down, only three men out of a crew of 1,419 survived.

the fight for a few more minutes. But many of her guns were not working, and German shells had already done serious damage. Six minutes after the first shot of the battle was fired, the British ship withdrew.

But the *Bismarck* had also been hurt. Three British shells had hit the German battleship. The most serious damage was forward where a shell had passed cleanly through the hull just above the water line. It was low enough that water thrown up by the bow was flowing right into the ship, flooding the forward compartments and cutting off access to the forward fuel tanks. The holes were patched over with collision mats, but there was nothing that could be done about the trapped fuel. As a result of her wounds the *Bismarck* could travel no faster than 28 knots, and her supply of available fuel was seriously reduced.

THE SINKING OF THE *HOOD*

1. A 15-inch (38-centimetre) shell from the *Bismarck* hits one of the magazines where explosives are stored.

2. The magazine explodes in a ball of fire, sending flames shooting into the sky.

3. The ship breaks in two and moments later sinks.

Continuing the *Bismarck*'s original mission was now out of the question. Reluctantly Admiral Lütjens decided to head for one of the ports in German-occupied France. Once repaired, the *Bismarck* would then be close to the sea lanes where most convoys sailed.

But first he had to get rid of the British ships still on his tail. As long as the British knew where he was, it was simply a matter of time before more warships intercepted him and forced him to fight. And next time he might not be so lucky.

Admiral Gunther Lütjens, the fleet commander.

May 25, 1941

"*Achtung, achtung.* Stand by for a message from the admiral."

It was almost noon as the loudspeakers blared. Instantly everyone on the *Bismarck* was wide awake. Many had recently heard talk that they had finally slipped away from the enemy. To escape his pursuers the admiral had steered the ship in a loop backwards across its own path. The crew now assumed the fleet commander was about to confirm the wonderful news that they were out of danger.

Then came Lütjens' formal clipped tones:

"Seamen of the battleship *Bismarck*! You have covered yourselves with glory! The sinking of the *Hood* was a great victory. But because of the hits we have received, we have been ordered to proceed to a French port. On our way there, the enemy will attempt to hunt us down and sink us. The German people are with you, and we will fight until our gun barrels glow red-hot. For us seamen, the question now is victory or death."

Victory or death. In the computer room Heinz, Franz and Adi looked at each other.

"What chance does a single ship have against the whole British navy?" Heinz asked, as much to himself as to anyone. No one responded. At his antiaircraft position, Alois heard the speech also. "We haven't got a hope," he muttered under his breath.

The only explanation for Lütjens' depressing speech was that even this late on May 25, nine hours after he had shaken off the British, the admiral still believed he was being followed.

The Atlantic Ocean, May 26, 1941

Alois was cold and tired. The antiaircraft crew had been in a state of constant alert since they had entered the Denmark Strait two and a half days ago. They had seldom left their battle stations during that time. But their spirits were high. More than twenty-four hours had passed since they had tried to shake off the British by looping backwards across their own path; perhaps they had escaped after all.

A gust of wind whipped through the open gun mount, and Alois shivered. When, he wondered, would he and his friends have a chance to relax and tell a few jokes. Admiral Lütjens with his talk of "victory or death" would make a great target for his mimicry. "'Seamen of the battleship *Bismarck*,'" he

After suffering shell hits during the battle, the *Bismarck*'s bow is low in the water.

The *Bismarck's* antiaircraft guns fire at the British Catalina flying boat as it suddenly appears beneath the clouds.

said to himself softly, practicing the admiral's clipped tones. He smiled as he imagined how he would have Adi, Franz and Heinz in stitches with his impression of the cold, stuck-up fleet commander. He was jolted back to reality as the aircraft alarm bells began to ring.

"Unidentified aircraft on the port quarter, bearing red one-nine-zero," shouted the section commander.

The gun mount swivelled rapidly until the two antiaircraft guns were pointing almost to the stern. Still Alois could see nothing. Suddenly an airplane that resembled a boat with wings broke through the clouds almost over the ship, and he began firing furiously. The noise was deafening. White puffs of smoke burst around the intruder, which banked hard and did violent S turns as it climbed back into the cloud cover. Alois cursed

to himself—and not just because they had failed to score any hits. The British had found them again for certain. Soon, he thought wearily, there would be another battle.

Now that contact had been reestablished, death, not victory, once again occupied the men's minds. As the hours passed the first British reconnaissance airplane was succeeded by another. By the time that one disappeared, a Swordfish biplane arrived on the scene and began shadowing the *Bismarck*. This meant that a British aircraft carrier with even more airplanes could not be far away.

For the rest of the day, as the German ship steamed

toward France, still trailing oil and now at the painfully slow speed of 20 knots, at least one British Swordfish was always on its tail. But they never came close enough for Alois and the other antiaircraft gunners to get a good shot at them. If the Germans had had more fuel they could have sailed faster, and by now might have been within range of protective aircraft from bases in occupied France. How Admiral Lütjens must have cursed himself for not topping up the *Bismarck*'s tanks in the Norwegian fjords when he'd had a chance.

Alois spent the rest of the day at his station on deck. The weather was getting worse, and he was often splashed with salt spray, which made him even colder. He and the rest of the crew took turns standing beside the nearby deck vent to warm up in the blast of hot air from the engines. But only for a minute. He expected a swarm of enemy torpedo bombers to swoop out of the clouds at any moment. But as dusk approached Alois began to relax a little. If the Brits hadn't attacked by now, they must have other plans. A nighttime battle perhaps?

Then, just before 9 p.m., when it seemed certain he would finally be able to go below for some food and warmth, the aircraft alarm bells began jangling again. Suddenly British planes were coming at the *Bismarck* from every direction, in ones and twos and threes, their wheels almost skimming the waves. In seconds, every gun on board the *Bismarck* was spitting fire.

Lieutenant-Commander Müllenheim-Rechberg could see the battle from his position high in the rear gunnery control station. The ship was in the midst of a high-speed turn to dodge oncoming torpedoes when he felt it tremble. His eyes automatically turned to the rudder indicator, and he waited for the ship to pull out of its turn. But nothing happened. The *Bismarck* stayed heeled heavily to starboard, and then began to slow down. Her rudders remained locked to port.

The *Bismarck* was now sailing back toward the chasing British fleet. Their magnificent new battleship, the pride of their navy that had struck so much fear into the enemy, was crippled and could not be steered.

It was now only a matter of time before the British would take revenge for the sinking of the *Hood*.

(Left) Flying just above the waves, a British Swordfish drops its torpedo on the *Bismarck*'s port side. At this level, the plane was too low to be hit by the *Bismarck*'s guns.
(Below) The torpedo from the Swordfish hit the *Bismarck*'s stern, damaging the rudders.

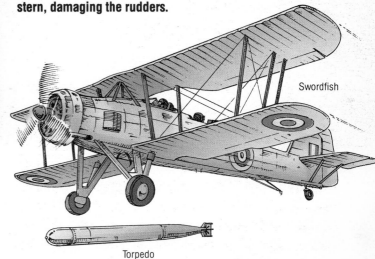

Swordfish

Torpedo

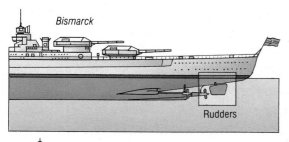

Bismarck

Rudders

The *Bismarck*'s line of fire

CHAPTER FOUR

The Bismarck's Last Stand

The Atlantic Ocean, May 27, 1941

I t was no use. All efforts to repair the *Bismarck*'s damaged rudders had failed. In the battle a torpedo from a British Swordfish had found the powerful ship's weakest spot. Now the best Captain Lindemann could do was sail slowly into the wind— away from France and back toward the enemy. As midnight passed and the storm worsened, everyone on board the German ship realized that the next battle would probably be their last. Although the men could not see them, they knew that British ships were gathering like sharks around a wounded whale. Through much of the night the *Bismarck*'s guns flashed fire as enemy destroyers moved in to launch torpedoes and enemy starshells burst overhead,

As the British ships close in, the *Bismarck*'s rear gun turrets, Caesar and Dora, flash defiantly through the night.

illuminating the battleship for the British gunners. But no shells or torpedoes found the mark. Clearly the British fleet was waiting until daylight to move in for the kill.

To the exhausted men in the rear computer room of the *Bismarck* this night battle served at least one useful purpose. It kept their minds off what lay ahead. But in the hours after midnight, as the British firing slackened, there were long periods when there was nothing to do. At one point when almost everyone was dozing at his station, catching a few precious minutes of sleep, the loudspeakers suddenly blared.

"*Achtung, achtung*. Men of the *Bismarck*, we have just received a message from Naval Command in Paris. U-boats are racing to join us. At dawn, eighty-one bombers will take off from France."

"Do you think the planes can get to us in time?" asked Franz.

"It'll be tough in such lousy weather," replied Adi. "But German pilots are the best. If anyone can, they can."

"And if they don't, we're done for," muttered Heinz to himself.

Soon the talk died down and the room was quiet. As tension ebbed, fatigue again took over. Franz began to snore.

"*Achtung, achtung*. A message from the Führer!" The loud-speakers jolted them wide awake again. "All Germany is with you. What can be done, will be done. Your performance of duty will strengthen our people in the strug-gle for its destiny."

There was a long silence before Heinz finally spoke.

"It's like he's saying goodbye. There must be no hope."

As Alois tried to sleep at his antiaircraft gun, his mind kept turning over the Führer's words. He wondered if he would soon be swimming in icy waters, far from friendly rescue.

Lieutenant-Commander Müllenheim-Rechberg, who spent the night in the gunnery control tower, was an experienced sailor. He knew that in this weather, this far from France, help was highly unlikely. But he kept these thoughts to himself. There was no sense in depressing his men.

He could not understand why the British had not attacked. It had been daylight for over an hour. What was the enemy waiting for? Since there was no use-ful job for him at his station, he headed for the bridge, hoping for some encouragement from the officers in charge. But the scene that greeted him there was

grim. No one talked and people stood or sat almost motionless. He saw to his astonishment that Captain Lindemann was wearing an open life jacket. The lieutenant walked over and saluted smartly, but the captain did not even return his salute and stared away blankly as he ate his breakfast in silence.

On his way back to his station, Müllenheim-Rechberg encountered Admiral Lütjens and his staff officer heading for the bridge. At least Lütjens met his gaze and returned his salute as he brushed past, but he too said nothing.

Seamen of the *Bismarck* usually ate together, but on the night before the final battle no one left his post.

As the *Bismarck* approached her final battle, the two men most responsible for her fate seemed to have withdrawn into private worlds.

Then the alarm bells rang out, and the young officer's unhappy thoughts vanished. He broke into a run. The battle was about to begin.

* * *

Two British battleships, glinting in the sunlight, charged toward the crippled German ship. From his battle station on deck, Alois scanned the horizon for enemy aircraft. Unbelievably there were none. Well, he thought, at least that gave them a chance. Even though the *Bismarck* was gravely wounded, her guns were still the best and her range finders the most skilled. The enemy ships were miles away, but coming in rapidly on their port bow, when their guns began to fire. First one salvo, then another. And just as in the battle with the *Hood*, it seemed like an eternity before his own ship returned fire. Finally Anton, Bruno, Caesar and Dora boomed their response, and Alois covered his ears against the noise. But worse was to come.

Although it was hopeless, he fired his puny antiaircraft gun at the enemy. At least it kept him occupied. Enemy shells whizzed overhead, but so far there had been no serious hits. Then a big shell slammed into the *Bismarck*, near turrets Anton and Bruno. The force of the blast almost blew him overboard. Fire flashed toward the bow, and Alois felt the ship shudder like a wounded animal. Grimly he waited for the *Bismarck*'s next salvo, but when it came only the rear guns fired: turrets Anton and Bruno had been knocked out of action. Hardly had this realization dawned on him than another British shell crashed into the ship destroying the foretop gunnery control station and taking with it the first gunnery officer. The battle had barely begun, but already the *Bismarck* was fighting with one eye blind and one arm broken.

Choking flames from the fire on the forward deck were now moving back toward the antiaircraft gunners, so the officer in charge ordered his men to evacuate their positions and head for the stern. Defiantly Alois fired a few final rounds at the enemy ships, now so close he imagined he could see the officers on their bridges. Then he followed his commander. While the battle raged, Alois and the rest of his crew found what shelter they could between turrets Caesar and Dora. And they waited.

Since the forward gunnery control station had been knocked out, Lieutenant-Commander Müllenheim-Rechberg in the rear gunnery control station had taken over direction of the battle. The defense of the *Bismarck* was now in his hands.

With his heart pounding he swept the horizon through his gun director until he got one of the British ships in his sights. It was less than seven miles

(Right) Admiral John Tovey in front of the big guns on the British battleship *King George V*, which fired on the *Bismarck*. (Bottom) A sailor loads shells to be fired from the guns of *King George V*.

(eleven kilometres) away.

"Fire one salvo," he ordered, and the *Bismarck* shook with the blast from its two rear turrets. He watched as the shell splashes rose like tall white fountains around the British ship.

He ordered three more salvos, but just after the last one straddled the enemy ship, the gun director shook violently and banged hard against his face. When Müllenheim-Rechberg looked again into the eyepiece all he could see was a blue blank. It had been shattered.

The *Bismarck* was now completely blind and all but helpless. There was nothing for the young officer to do but let turrets Caesar and Dora fire independently. The battle was less than half an hour old.

Salvos from British ships splash all around the *Bismarck* as it fights for its life in the final hour. With its damaged rudders, the ship was crippled even before the battle began.

Deep inside the *Bismarck*, in the boiler rooms and engine rooms, it was impossible to distinguish between the thud of the *Bismarck*'s guns and the explosion of British shells hitting the ship. But whenever a shell splashed near the hull, cold, green seawater poured in through the air intake shafts. In other positions below decks, in the computer rooms, the infirmaries, the magazines and the galleys, the men knew only what their officers told them. Each battle station was isolated from the next one, and the only contact with other parts of the ship was by telephone. Soon the telephone lines were damaged and almost all communication stopped. But still the men toiled on or waited for orders that never came. For many in the forward part of the ship where damage was the greatest, death came swiftly.

The two enemy ships were now so close that the battle was turning into target practice for the British. Shell after shell slammed into the *Bismarck*. Soon the forward part of the ship was an almost total wreck, with fires raging and smoke billowing upward, but her two rear turrets continued to fire. Finally, after only forty-five minutes of fighting, the *Bismarck*'s last two gun turrets were blasted into silence. Her gun barrels now drooped like wilted flowers, but still the British poured their fire into the burning, smoking hulk.

Shortly after the *Bismarck* fired its final salvo, the telephone rang in the engine room where Lieutenant-Commander Gerhard Junack, the chief turbine officer, was at the post he had not left for more than a day.

"Prepare to scuttle," said the chief engineer.

"Aye, aye, sir," replied Junack. This was an order he had prayed he would never hear. It meant letting water flow into all parts of the ship so that it would sink as quickly as possible. Lütjens had decided the *Bismarck* could not fall into enemy hands.

Quickly Junack inspected the engine room to make sure that all the doors were open so that water could pass between watertight compartments. He ordered his chief machinist to ignite the fuses to the scuttling explosives. Then he left his station with the last of his men.

In the computer room it was getting stuffy. Heinz, Adi and Franz sat silently at their positions, waiting for the young lieutenant who was in charge to do something. The telephone had stopped working but the ship's alarm bells continued to ring loudly. The lights flickered occasionally. There was nothing for them to do since their own guns had ceased

The guns on the British battleship *Rodney* (below) fired at the *Bismarck*, creating fountain-like shell splashes in the water as shown in the photograph (inset) taken during the battle.

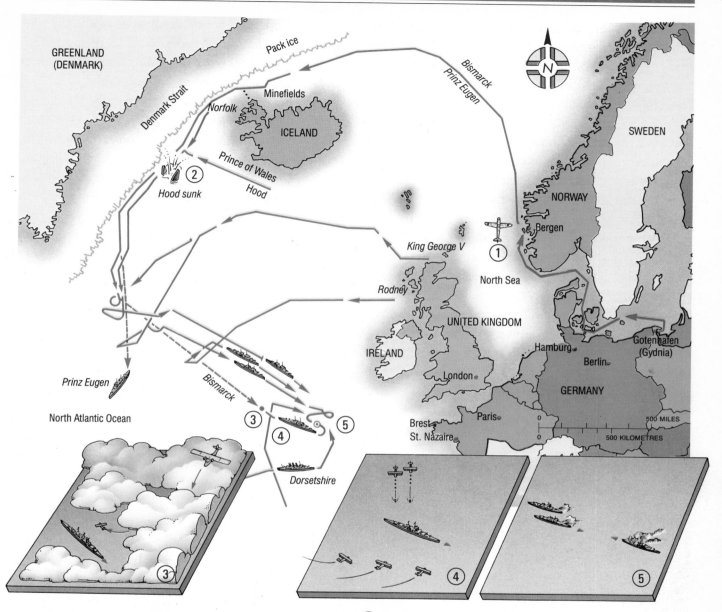

This map shows the paths of the *Bismarck* and *Prinz Eugen* and the major British ships involved in the chase and final sea battle.

① **May 21, 1941:** A Spitfire spots the German battleships in the Norwegian fjords.

② **May 24:** The *Bismarck* sinks the *Hood*.

③ **May 26:** More than twenty-four hours after the *Bismarck* has disappeared, a Catalina flying boat finds her again.

④ **May 26:** Two Swordfish biplanes approach on the port side and launch torpedoes. One of them hits the *Bismarck*'s rudders.

⑤ **May 27:** The final battle. British ships close in, firing on the burning *Bismarck*.

firing, but they could hear the distant rumble each time an enemy shell hit the *Bismarck*. They were scared. Soon their ship would start sinking and they would be trapped. But they could not leave their posts until ordered to do so.

Heinz felt a ticking in his ears. The air pressure was increasing. Perhaps the ship was already going down, taking them with it. He fought back panic, and

without asking permission lay down on the floor; the ticking stopped. Finally the lieutenant sent someone to find out what was going on. A few minutes later the man reported back that the order had already gone out to scuttle and abandon ship.

"All right men, follow me." The lieutenant's quavering voice sounded much less confident than his words. He was as frightened as they were.

"Do I have time to go to my quarters?" asked Franz, who was thinking of his personal belongings.

"Don't be crazy," replied Heinz sharply. "The ship is sinking!"

The lieutenant led the way along the narrow, empty corridor to the door leading to stairs. But when he opened the door he found choking black smoke and flames. Quickly he slammed it shut. His face was white and his hands were shaking. He seemed paralyzed. The men looked at each other nervously. They were trapped.

"The cable shaft," said Heinz pointing to the nearby entry hatch to the shaft that carried cables between the computer room and the gunnery control station high above. Adi and Franz quickly moved to help their friend, while the others, including the lieutenant, watched and waited. The hatch seemed to be welded in place—then suddenly, with a creak it wrenched open.

"I'm not going up that way," one of them called out. "That's suicide." Several others nodded.

Heinz took one last look at the group of men gathered in the corridor, before climbing into the dark. For a moment he couldn't breathe. Then he forced himself to take in a long deep breath. The air was stale, but clean. He began to breathe more easily. He found the first rung of a ladder and began to climb. He heard noises behind him, but he had no way of knowing how many of his comrades had decided to follow.

In darkness Heinz climbed until he could climb no further. Groping blindly he found the hatch handle. It was directly above his head, but it wouldn't budge. Finally he took the housing from his gas mask and banged on the metal. If someone was alive up there, they would hear him. It was getting hot in the narrow shaft, breathing was becoming difficult, and sweat

When Adi, Heinz, Franz and the other men in the computer room discovered that the stairs to the next deck up were blocked by flames, they were forced to escape by climbing up a cable shaft leading to the gunnery control station.

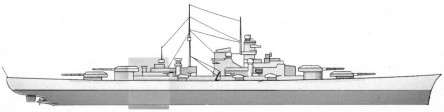

poured down his face and stung his eyes. Then he heard the sound of scraping, the latch was released, and the hatch opened.

Heinz blinked at the brightness as a slimy liquid poured down on him, making it difficult to get himself into the room. Hands reached down and pulled him up. Then he realized that he was drenched in blood. The floor was covered with it. Its awful smell filled his nostrils and he fought back the urge to throw up as he looked around the crowded room. First Franz, then Adi followed him through the hatch. Then came the lieutenant and one other. But that was all.

They were in the gunnery control station commanded by Müllenheim-Rechberg. Now it was full of men who had escaped from the lower decks and were waiting for the British guns to stop firing. Some of them were badly wounded. Some were dead.

Suddenly there was a loud explosion nearby and stinging yellow smoke filled the room. As the men automatically reached for their gas masks, Franz grabbed Heinz's shoulder.

"I've lost my mask!" he blurted out in a terrified voice as he began to cough from the fumes.

"Here." Heinz ripped a mask away from a dead man and handed it to him. Franz put it on and waited for the smoke to clear.

Suddenly Heinz felt liquid dripping inside his mask. He touched his forehead. It was wet with blood —he had been wounded. His heart pounded heavily. He felt the urge to rip off his gas mask, but he forced himself to remain calm. Finally some hatches were opened and the men could remove their masks.

Lieutenant-Commander Müllenheim-Rechberg *(inset)* was in command of the rear gunnery control station *(above)* to which many fled from the lower decks.

"How bad is it?" he asked Franz, pointing to his wound.

"Nothing, a scratch," replied his friend. A shell splinter from the explosion had grazed Heinz's forehead. He had been lucky. One person in the room had been killed.

They waited until British shells stopped hitting the ship. As the shell-shocked sailors frantically pushed their way out of the small room, Heinz became separated from his friends. He was dazed as the smoke swirled around him, but he was too tired now to feel panic. The deck of the *Bismarck* was a scene of complete devastation—mangled steel, gaping shell holes and fires burning everywhere. But the blood that made the deck slippery, the dead bodies, the screams and moans from injured men seemed ghostly, unreal. He found a sheltered spot and sat down to have a smoke.

Finally Heinz decided it was time to move. The slope of the deck was increasing. If he didn't leave

the ship soon, it would leave him. Calmly he removed his boots and took off his uniform so that he was only wearing his socks and his longjohns. He put on his lifejacket and inflated it. Then he slid into the water.

After Heinz and most of the others had left, Franz and Adi continued to stand on the platform outside the gunnery control station. The stairs down to

Captain Lindemann went down with the *Bismarck*.

the next deck level were gone.

"I can't jump that far," argued Franz. "I'll break my leg."

"Better break your leg than lose your life," shot back Adi, but still Franz hesitated. "We don't have all day, Franz," he insisted impatiently. "Follow me."

Adi jumped, landing on a dead body, which cushioned his fall. To Franz that seemed even worse. He stood there, frozen.

"Come on," shouted his friend. "Jump!"

Franz closed his eyes, took a deep breath and leaped into the air. The next thing he knew he'd crashed onto a bundle of something lumpy and hard. When he opened his eyes he discovered it was a sack of potatoes. He felt his arms and legs. Nothing seemed broken. Then he saw a group of men gathered near turret Dora, and he headed for them. Among them was Alois, blackened from the battle but still able to flash him a grin of recognition.

The only officer in this group was Lieutenant-Commander Müllenheim-Rechberg, who was speaking to the men.

"We're sinking slowly. The sea is running high and we'll have to swim a long time. Wait as long as possible before jumping. I'll tell you when. Some ships will surely come along and pick us up."

Several of the sailors muttered rebelliously, but no one made a move. Before long the ship's tilt to port became alarming.

"All right, men. Inflate your lifejackets," shouted Müllenheim-Rechberg. "Prepare to abandon ship." He looked up and saw that the *Bismarck*'s battle standard was still flying from the mainmast. "A salute to our fallen comrades," he called out. Then he saluted the flag and jumped.

In the water, hundreds of men were swimming for their lives, struggling to get clear of the ship's powerful suction as it went down. But some turned

to watch the *Bismarck*'s final moments. Heinz could see the bow of the ship and was astonished to observe Captain Lindemann standing on the deck in front of turret Anton. With him was the young seaman who had acted as his messenger.

How had the captain survived the raging furnace that had enveloped the forward part of the ship? As the slope of the deck increased, the two figures moved toward the bow: it was obvious from Lindemann's gestures that he was trying to persuade the young man to jump, to save himself, but he refused. As the ship turned on its side, the two walked out onto the hull and then, as it turned over, stood on the keel. Then Lindemann saluted and the *Bismarck* went down.

Hundreds of German sailors now found themselves floating in the choppy sea. Surprisingly, many didn't notice that the water was near freezing. Those who did felt it first in their hands and feet—one man who had lost his socks felt his legs go numb. Heinz

The damaged *Bismarck* tilts heavily to port in the final moments of the battle.

had kept his socks, but soon began to regret his decision to strip down to his longjohns. Far worse than the cold was the fuel oil, which lay in a horrible stinking slick over the waves and got into the eyes and noses of the sailors.

The men had been in the water for about an hour when they saw the silhouette of a three-stack cruiser—the *Dorsetshire*. They began to swim toward salvation as British sailors lowered lines—the sea was too rough to launch boats. Soon the sheltered side of the British ship was crowded with hundreds of men desperately trying to get on board. The oil made the ropes slippery and the cold cramped their hands—it was almost impossible for most to hold on unless the rope was tied with a loop on the end—then they could get a foot or an arm through. Müllenheim-Rechberg

found a loop, stepped in and was within a few feet of safety when he released one hand to reach out for another line. Before he could grab on, his other hand gave way and he fell back into the sea. The second time he held tight the whole way. When he reached deck level he said politely in his best English, "Please pull me on board."

Franz did not fare so well. He tried and failed to grab a line from the *Dorsetshire*. Then he saw a British destroyer off in the distance and swam toward

In the black oily sea, men from the *Bismarck* cling to ropes lowered from the British cruiser *Dorsetshire*. Many sailors were too badly injured to make it on board.

it. It took him three tries to get on board, and he was so exhausted that two sailors had to drag him over the railing.

When Heinz finally made it onto the *Dorsetshire* a friendly sailor handed him a bottle of rum. The liquor tasted like fire and burned his throat, and when it hit his stomach he threw up violently. But at least this emptied him of the oily seawater he had swallowed. Someone draped a blanket over his shoulders and led him below. When he reached the room that had been turned into an infirmary for German sailors, he discovered that Adi was already there.

Many were less lucky. One man whose arms had been blown off was trying to grab a line in his teeth. Aboard the *Dorsetshire*, a seventeen-year-old midshipman climbed over the side in an attempt to help him, when the ship unexpectedly began to move forward. The British sailor lost him, and he only barely managed to climb back on board himself.

The rescue had barely begun but one of the officers aboard the *Dorsetshire* had spotted movement in the ocean a few miles away. Was it a German U-boat? The two British ships were perfect targets sitting dead in the water. There seemed no choice but to get under way as quickly as possible. As the ships began to gather speed, men still in the water clung desperately to lines, while others scratched uselessly at the gray paint as the ship slid past. Only those who were already partway up a rope had a chance. Hundreds of others watched in disbelief from the water as their only hope quickly faded into the distance. Theirs would be a slow, creeping death.

The men pulled from the water were so blackened with oil they looked like coal miners. Lieutenant-Commander Müllenheim-Rechberg was the highest ranking of the four officers to survive. Lieutenant-Commander Gerhard Junack, who had scuttled the ship, also made it to safety. Antiaircraft gunner Alois Haberditz was also pulled up on board the *Dorsetshire*. In all, only 115 men survived out of a crew of 2,206.

* * *

On May 28, one of the rescued German sailors died on board the *Dorsetshire*. He had been badly burned and had lost an arm: it was amazing he had made it so far. The next day British and German sailors who had so recently been trying to kill each other gathered on the deck for the funeral. At first Heinz, Adi and Alois, who couldn't speak any English, didn't understand what was happening. But then they saw the body wrapped in the ensign of the Imperial German Navy, noticed the honor guard from the *Dorsetshire*, and saw the chaplain in his robes. All at once they realized that the British were burying the German sailor with full military honors.

While a bugler played the last post, the German and British sailors stood solemnly at attention. Then the Germans were permitted to give the Nazi salute. Finally one of the *Bismarck*'s crew played a sad sailor's lament on a borrowed harmonica: "*Ich hatt' einen Kameraden*" or "I had a comrade." Heinz, Adi and Alois had already lost so many friends. As the body was committed to the waves, they wept. As they

Survivors arrive at a British port. Franz Halke is at the bottom of the gangway.

did, they noticed that many of the British sailors were crying too.

Adi Eich, Heinz Jucknat, Franz Halke, Alois Haberditz and Burkard von Müllenheim-Rechberg would spend the next few years as prisoners of war. But that day as they stood on the deck of the *Dorsetshire* they were just happy to be alive.

Nowhere in their wildest imaginings did it occur to any of the survivors that they would ever see the *Bismarck* again.

CHAPTER FIVE

Discovery!

The Atlantic Ocean, May 30, 1989

On the *Star Hercules* (above) Hagen Schempf and I discuss our strategy for finding the *Bismarck*.

"Dad, we're ready for the launch."

Todd's voice brought me back to the present with a jolt. I had been deeply engrossed in a description of the sinking of the *Bismarck* written by one of the survivors, Lieutenant-Commander Müllenheim-Rechberg.

"I'll be right there," I said.

We had spent our first day in the search area positioning transponders—underwater acoustic beacons that permit us to navigate *Argo* with pinpoint precision. Now we were ready to begin our hunt for the German battleship. I left my cabin and went out to the fantail of the *Star Hercules*, where my team was preparing to launch *Argo*.

In rough weather, launches and recoveries can be dangerous. When *Argo* starts to swing from its giant yellow A-frame, it becomes a two-ton wrecking ball. Fortunately the weather was calm and the sun was shining as we hoisted the white-painted sled over the stern. Our camera vehicle would take three hours to fall the three-mile (5-kilometre) distance to the bottom of the ocean.

Somewhere far below our ship, in the dark and the cold where no sunlight ever penetrates, lay the remains of the *Bismarck*. Was it in one piece or scattered across the ocean floor? I have looked at several wrecks over the years. Some are almost perfectly preserved time capsules, others piles of junk. Given the pummelling the *Bismarck* took, it seemed unlikely she would much resemble her former lethal self. But by all eyewitness accounts she had left the surface in one piece.

Now that we were about to go into action I could sense the rising excitement among the crew. Home and solid ground seemed a million miles away as all our thoughts turned to the challenge ahead.

One of the biggest problems with finding the wreck was that the British ships that took part in the *Bismarck*'s last battle left three different sinking positions. And so the search area was huge—almost 200 square miles (520 square kilometres) of empty ocean. To make matters worse, most of this area was dominated by a massive group of underwater volcanoes rising up from the ocean floor. Their ridges and gullies would make it a real challenge to drive *Argo* without crashing. Because of this rough terrain we planned to fly *Argo* only ten to fifteen metres above the bottom so that its video cameras could pick up even the smallest item of man-made debris.

Every shipwreck leaves a debris trail as it sinks: the lighter pieces of debris are carried further by the underwater currents than the heavier pieces of the ship. The

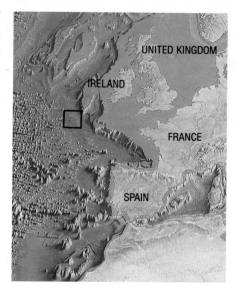

The black outline on the map *(above)* shows our *Bismarck* search area in the Atlantic Ocean. You can see many seamounts, or underwater mountains, rising from the ocean floor.

further they fall, the more spread out the debris trail becomes. Because of the depth—three miles (five kilometres)—I was sure the *Bismarck* would have left a debris trail at least a mile long.

My strategy was simple: look for the debris trail, not the ship. To do this I would run east/west search lines one mile apart. If the ship had sunk inside our search area, we were bound to run across a piece of its debris sooner or later.

But it wasn't going to be easy. I've often compared an underwater search to looking for a needle in a haystack at night, in a blizzard, with nothing more than a flashlight. At least *Argo* is a very expensive, high-tech flashlight.

Argo reached the bottom at 9 a.m., and I instructed the navigator to begin our first search line. As the *Star Hercules* began moving slowly eastward, Kirk, flying *Argo*, watched the video

Todd lends a hand as we haul *Argo* aboard from the fantail of the *Star Hercules*.

screen in front of him which showed the view from *Argo*'s forward-looking camera. In one corner of the screen a digital display indicated *Argo*'s altitude above the bottom. At the same time he was paying attention to the return from *Argo*'s sonar, which would warn him long before his cameras that an obstacle lay ahead. Kirk's job was to compensate for the swell at the surface and any changes in the bottom to maintain a steady altitude. It was a good thing that he and his buddies were fine athletes; flying *Argo* requires excellent co-ordination and reflexes.

"I'm getting a soft contact on the forward sonar," called out the sonar operator. That meant he was getting a faint echo from an object up ahead.

"Get ready to come up, Kirk," I ordered.

We were now approaching the western slope of one of the underwater volcanoes. As it neared, I could see Kirk tense a little. He leaned forward and his grip on the joystick tightened. We were all wondering just how steep it would be.

"Come up," I said. "Gently, not too fast."

As we hit the slope Kirk's reflexes responded instantly. He eased back on the joystick and brought *Argo* up slowly, but fast enough to keep us well above the bottom. I relaxed. Kirk didn't seem to be having any trouble keeping up with the rising altitude, and the bottom continued smooth and sediment covered, revealing none of the dangerous volcanic outcrops I'd feared.

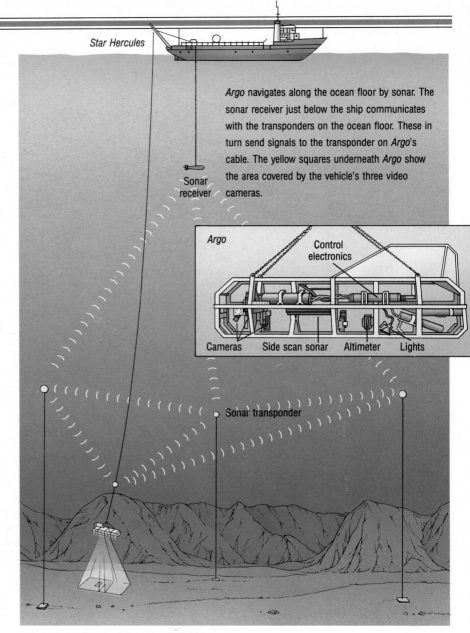

Star Hercules

Argo navigates along the ocean floor by sonar. The sonar receiver just below the ship communicates with the transponders on the ocean floor. These in turn send signals to the transponder on *Argo*'s cable. The yellow squares underneath *Argo* show the area covered by the vehicle's three video cameras.

Sonar receiver

Argo

Control electronics

Cameras   Side scan sonar   Altimeter   Lights

Sonar transponder

With his hand on the joystick and his eyes on the video screens, Kirk "flies" *Argo* over the ocean floor.

June 2, 1989

By the fourth day of our search for the *Bismarck* we'd seen rocky outcrops but only a few scattered pieces of man-made debris. All of it was near the spot that the navigator aboard the *Dorsetshire*, the ship that rescued the majority of *Bismarck* survivors, had estimated as the battleship's sinking position. But we had found no debris trail, and definitely no ship.

I looked down at the *Argo* station where Billy Yunck was preparing to turn the joystick over to Todd. The three young flyers were doing a good job, but I knew the monotony of our fruitless search was getting to them. They weren't used to being cooped up like this. Cabin fever was a real possibility.

Soon the new watch had settled in. Apart from the music playing softly on the stereo, the only sounds were the background hum of the ventilator fans and the sonar printer. Everyone on board was waiting for something—anything—to happen.

The video log told the story of our expedition so far. A series of typical entries looked like this: "12:21—fish; 13:03—octopod; 14:42—black rock." It

After endless hours of staring at nothing but mud on our video screens, we begin to feel like zombies and wonder if we will ever find the Bismarck.

certainly wasn't much to write home about.

At least Hagen Schempf, the watch leader, was good at keeping up his troops' morale. In his late twenties, he was the youngest of the three watch leaders. He was the only German citizen on board, and the *Bismarck* story fascinated him.

"Well, I'm going outside to get some fresh air," I announced. "Hagen, give me a shout if anything interesting turns up." I wasn't expecting much, however. As we crossed back and forth over the search area, it was beginning to seem more and more unlikely that there was a ship down there to find.

June 5, 1989

After seven days of deep ocean search, Billy, Todd and Kirk weren't the only ones going crazy with the close quarters and the numbing routine of life at sea. Even the veterans on the team were starting to look glassy-eyed. If we didn't find something soon, I thought, we might all turn into zombies. By now we'd covered three-quarters of our search area and found nothing. My troops were beginning to wonder if I had led them on a wild goose chase.

Inside the control van Todd and Hagen's watch was on duty. I looked on as my son expertly piloted *Argo* over the underwater hills and valleys that lay three miles (five kilometres) below.

We work and store our equipment inside these huge vans on the deck of the *Star Hercules*. At the stern of the ship is the giant yellow A-frame from which we raise and lower *Argo*.

When Todd's watch ended he and I went outside and walked aft to the raised platform at the stern of the *Star Hercules*. It was a perfect place to stand and talk, or watch the sunset.

"Maybe the *Bismarck* has disappeared into a black hole," I began. "I'm beginning to wonder if we're ever going to find it."

"Don't worry, Dad. You'll find it. You always do."

When the evening air began to chill, Todd headed to his cabin and I went to the mess hall, where a group was waiting to play Trivial Pursuit. I sat down, opened a Coke, popped a handful of potato chips in my mouth, and settled in for a couple of hours of diversion. Dice rolled and markers moved along the board. In a matter of minutes the battleship *Bismarck* couldn't have been further from my thoughts.

But then I heard a voice over my shoulder.

"Bob, we've encountered some debris I think you should have a look at."

I jumped out of my seat, vaulting over the banquette in one motion as potato chips and Trivial Pursuit pieces scattered in every direction. I ran full tilt for the control van, leaving everyone else far behind me.

When I reached the van a clump of small black objects was just coming into view on the video screens. Although to an inexperienced eye they might have looked like nothing more than dark smudges on the sediment, there was no doubt that they were pieces of man-made material.

"Looks like we've got something this time," commented the watch leader.

"Yeah, absolutely no doubt about it," I replied. "But what? If it's the *Bismarck*, we've got two choices. Either this stuff was shot off during the final battle, or this is part of the debris field."

"We're not picking up any sonar contacts on the sidescan," reported the sonar operator.

"What's that?" I asked as a larger piece of debris loomed onto the video screen. "Zoom in on that. Let's take a closer look."

The *Argo* engineer's fingers flew over his keyboard, instantly sending instructions along the cable, ordering *Argo*'s zoom camera to close in. The object looked like a piece of pipe, but it was difficult to be sure.

When I'd arrived the van was already crowded. It was a few minutes before midnight and a watch change was in progress. Now the film crew from National Geographic television, on board to make a documentary movie about our expedition, rolled in with cameras and sound gear and started to set up. Soon the long narrow room was bursting.

Usually, when a new shift takes over, the previous watch disappears fairly quickly, but not tonight. Almost everyone hung around, wanting to be in on the big moment when we found the wreck. All eyes were glued to the video screens and although voices were hushed, everyone was excited. The monotony was finally over.

With the *Star Hercules* at dead

(Above) A sonar printout shows us the ground that *Argo* has covered so far. *(Below)* I look at the video screens closely, trying to identify the pieces of debris *Argo*'s cameras have just picked up.

slow, we headed east and continued to pick up occasional pieces of debris. I was more and more sure that we had found a genuine debris field associated with a wreck, not just a few pieces shot off during a running battle.

But was it the right wreck? And what was the meaning of the strange churned-up bottom we had suddenly begun to pass over? It looked as though rocks and sediment had been put through a blender. Where had I seen this kind of thing before?

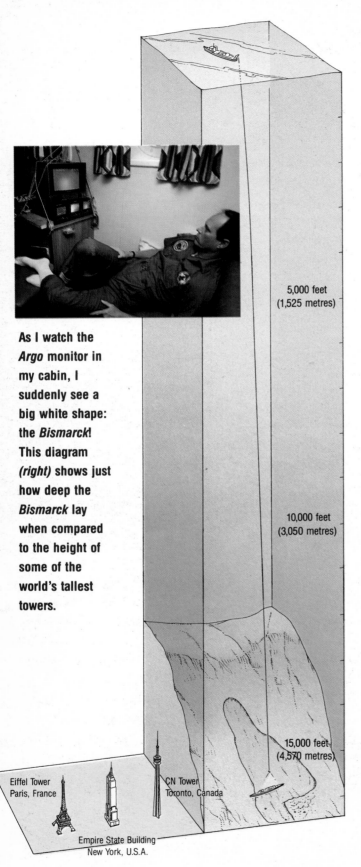

As I watch the *Argo* monitor in my cabin, I suddenly see a big white shape: the *Bismarck*! This diagram (right) shows just how deep the *Bismarck* lay when compared to the height of some of the world's tallest towers.

5,000 feet
(1,525 metres)

10,000 feet
(3,050 metres)

15,000 feet
(4,570 metres)

Eiffel Tower
Paris, France

Empire State Building
New York, U.S.A.

CN Tower
Toronto, Canada

Then my heart started to beat faster as I finally figured it out. We had discovered a huge underwater landslide, and I knew only one thing could have caused an avalanche this big—the *Bismarck*!

June 8, 1989

I snapped awake with a start, sat up in my bunk, and grabbed my watch. It was after 9 a.m., but I was still tired. Our search was turning into a real marathon. In the two days since we'd found the first debris I'd hardly slept at all. So far we'd discovered all sorts of wreckage and even a big gun turret upside down in the mud. That told us the *Bismarck* was definitely nearby, but we still didn't know where, and time was running out. In four days we would have to pack up and head home.

Reluctantly, I pulled on some clothes. Maybe I would take it easy just a bit longer, I thought. By simply watching the video monitors installed in my cabin I could see everything my team was watching in the control van.

I flopped down on the couch and turned my gaze to the *Argo* monitor. This showed me what our robot was seeing as it moved along the ocean floor. Kirk's watch was on duty. I imagined him sitting at the *Argo* station, his eyes fixed on the monitor and its altitude reading, one hand resting lightly on the joystick. The landslide, with its tricky slopes and outcrops and scattered debris was challenging terrain. I lay back on the couch and watched with pleasure as Kirk skilfully glided the vehicle over the rugged landscape.

Suddenly a big white shape loomed into the view of *Argo*'s forward-looking camera. How would Kirk handle this one? I was almost chuckling as I watched him react in a split second and begin reeling in cable.

Then I saw the gun—no, two gun barrels jutting from a turret.

"We've got it!" I yelled, so loud that I was heard two corridors away.

By the time I burst into the control van, *Argo* had passed over the wreck, but the *Argo* engineer was ready to replay the discovery sequence. "Look at that baby!" I exclaimed. "We've got it! We've got it! All right!"

Word spread rapidly through the ship, and soon the van was packed. Todd and Billy were among the

ALT 12.4 HD 060.8

(Top) When I saw this picture of a gun turret with two barrels pointing from it, I was convinced we had found the wreck.
(Above) The team inside the control van was tired but happy that our long search was successful.

first to arrive. They both congratulated Kirk, but I could tell they were envious.

"How much did our shift miss it by, Dad?" Todd asked me as we watched the video one more time.

"About thirty metres," I told him. I had checked our coverage and seen that we had barely missed the main wreck several times. I could see Todd's disappointment, mixed with pride and elation.

Whatever happened now, our *Bismarck* expedition was a success. I felt as though a great pressure had suddenly been released. All at once the *Bismarck* story came pouring into my head. As I stared at those mute guns and the blasted superstructure, the awful last hours of the German battleship were suddenly real, not simply buried inside history books.

Young men had lived on this ship, fought bravely for her during her hopeless final battle, and died.

CHAPTER SIX

Exploring the Sunken Wreck

The Atlantic Ocean, June 8, 1989

We were about to take our first close look at the mighty *Bismarck*, unseen by human eyes for almost fifty years. Billy Yunck's watch was on duty in the control van, and there were quite a few spectators. No one who was awake wanted to miss the show.

"All right, let's see what kind of shape she's in," I said. "Billy, go down slowly."

Billy pushed forward on the joystick and the altitude reading began to decrease: 50 metres, 45 metres, 40 metres, 35 metres.

We were coming in directly over the wreck, like a helicopter dropping down over an enemy position. About 30 metres from the bottom a ghostly gray form materialized dimly in the murky distance.

"Okay, bring her down gently." The wind on the surface had been picking up for the past couple of hours, and *Argo* was rising and falling as much as several metres with each swell. The last thing I needed right now was a crash landing.

Gradually the murk thinned and the details of the picture on the video monitors came into focus. First we saw an undamaged gun turret, then horribly mangled metal plating where a shell had hit.

Our goal was to videotape and photograph every inch of the sunken ship. As the hours passed, a clearer picture of the wreck began to emerge. It was a strange mixture of destruction and preservation. Many guns were still in place, but there were some huge holes in the deck and some of the upper parts of the ship had been completely blasted away.

At 4 p.m. sharp Todd's watch relieved Billy's. In the three hours that we'd been working over the wreck the surface weather had been getting steadily worse, and the flyer's job was becoming more difficult by the minute. But Todd was an expert at counteracting the rise and fall of the *Star Hercules*. As the ship fell he would raise *Argo*; as it rose he would lower it. This worked well until we hit a deep trough between waves where the ship fell and then fell further, instead of going up again. A few times we came close to crashing.

Todd, at the *Argo* controls, guides our camera vehicle three miles (five kilometres) below as we explore the eerie wreck of the *Bismarck*.

As we approached the rear gunnery control station I sensed an extra level of anticipation in the van. We had all read the *Bismarck* story and we knew that this was where Lieutenant-Commander Burkard von Müllenheim-Rechberg had spent the battle. This was also the place where so many of those who survived the sinking had sought shelter, including the three friends from the rear gunnery computer room — Adi Eich, Franz Halke and Heinz Jucknat.

The station was intact. It was amazing that it had survived the battle so well, since it was not a heavily armored structure.

Now we headed aft, past the round gaping mouths where turrets Caesar and Dora had once sat.

The swastika on the bow deck reminded us that the *Bismarck* was a Nazi warship.

None of the four big turrets was still attached to the ship. Soon we were out over empty decking and approaching the stern.

"Stop! What's that?" I said. *Argo*'s video cameras had just picked up some dark markings on the ship.

"It's a cross," said a voice behind me.

"No," I said, looking intently at the screen. "No, that's not a cross. It's a swastika."

"Of course, the swastika!" exclaimed Hagen, half to himself. *(continued on page 58)*

The Port Side of the Ship

Argo's lights shine on antiaircraft guns that look ready to fire again *(above)*. The photograph *(right)*, taken before the *Bismarck* embarked on her secret mission, shows the same area of the ship before it was damaged in battle.

1. Swastika on the bow deck

2. Anchor chain lying in a shell hole

3. Remains of gun turret Anton

4. Remains of gun turret Bruno

5. 37-millimetre (1.5-inch) antiaircraft guns

6. Blasted remains of the open bridge

7. Roof of the conning tower

8. 150-millimetre (5.9-inch) antiaircraft guns

9. Huge shell hole

10. Roof of the rear gunnery control station where Lieutenant-Commander Müllenheim-Rechberg conducted the last stages of the battle.

11. Remains of gun turret Caesar

12. Remains of gun turret Dora

The Forward Deck

The *Bismarck*'s anchor chain once stretched neatly toward the bow *(left)*. But as the underwater pictures *(above)* show, the anchor chain now disappears down a large shell hole. You can still see the teak planks from which the deck was made.

The Starboard Side of the Ship

When we explored the starboard side of the wreck *(right)* we could see the door that Adolf Hitler walked through when he visited the *Bismarck* on May 5, 1941 *(above)*.

The Forward Part of the Ship

The forward part of the *Bismarck* today looks much as it did when the ship was being built as seen in the photograph *(left)*. Much of the open bridge, from which the ship was directed, was blasted away during the battle. But you can still see parts of the bridge to the left of the conning tower *(above)*, the area from which the ship was steered.

Antiaircraft Guns

The haunting underwater photograph *(below)* shows the *Bismarck*'s antiaircraft guns decorated with sea anemones. Identical guns can be seen in the 1941 photograph *(left)*.

The Stern of the Ship

This painting of the *Bismarck* on the ocean floor *(top)*, shows where the tip of the stern broke away from the ship as it sank. In the photograph *(above)* Adolf Hitler stands on the swastika near the point where the stern tore free. An underwater photograph *(below)* shows the jagged edge where the break took place.

How the *Bismarck* Sank

1. Toward the end of the battle the stern begins to sink.

2. Just before sinking, the ship rolls over and the bow points into the air. The gun turrets and other pieces of debris fall to the ocean floor, and the stern breaks off.

3. With the hull now full of water, the *Bismarck* falls slowly toward the bottom of the ocean.

4. With all the air gone from the ship, it rights itself and continues to fall more quickly.

5. About ten to twenty minutes after leaving the surface, the hull hits an underwater mountain causing a huge landslide.

6. The avalanche carries the ship and other heavy pieces of wreckage down the slope.

(continued from page 51)

The van went silent. In our excitement we'd forgotten just what we were looking at: a Nazi warship. Suddenly all the evil associations that went with the Nazi symbol ran through our minds: the invasions which led to the outbreak of World War II bringing widespread death and destruction, the concentration camps and the millions of people murdered there. My mind went back to the day Hitler came on

This rope wreath was made by one of the crewmen for our memorial service.

board to inspect his new battleship before her first mission. I wondered how differently the war might have turned out if the *Bismarck* had broken into the Atlantic to attack ships transporting food and supplies to the islands of Great Britain.

Although the swastikas on the bow and stern decks had been painted over when the *Bismarck* headed for the Atlantic, after forty-eight years the seawater had gradually worn that paint away.

As we moved further aft, the swastika suddenly sheared away as if chopped by a guillotine.

"That took one heck of a karate chop," I said.

"Wow!" said Todd. "Do you think that was caused by a torpedo?"

"If so, no one saw it happen when the ship was still at the surface," I replied.

As we moved off the stern we glimpsed rubble down below, but there was no sign of the vanished chunk of hull.

For almost five hours we beetled our way along the deck of the ravaged ship, awed by the damage yet marveling at how much remained, how powerful and proud the ship still looked. I wondered what the survivors would think when they saw the pictures of the *Bismarck* again after so long.

June 12, 1989

"Being gathered here today gives us the opportunity to remember those young British and German seamen who lost their lives during the days of this tragic sea battle..." The stern deck of the *Star Hercules* was crowded with people. Almost everyone on board had turned out for a memorial service organized by Hagen Schempf and conducted by the captain of the *Star Hercules*. The weather was beautiful—bright warm sun and a gentle wind. The storm that had made our last days on site so difficult was now a distant memory.

I looked around the deck. The officers were in their dress uniforms and the rest of us had done our best to make ourselves presentable, but we were a motley crew: during our weeks at sea, beards had gone unshaven, hair uncut. Todd and his friends stood together, listening quietly.

"...let us hope that this kind of human suffering and sacrifice may

In a nearby debris field *Argo*'s cameras picked up the chilling image of a boot on the ocean floor, reminding us of the many young men who went down with the *Bismarck*.

never be asked of mankind again."

The captain called for a minute of silence. I glanced over at Hagen and wondered what he was thinking. Finding the wreck had brought him face to face with a piece of his own history. He didn't talk about it, but it was obvious to anyone who knew him well that he had been deeply affected by the experience.

And he was not alone. It was impossible to look at the ghostly wreck or the many boots scattered in the nearby debris field and not think of the young men, most of them no older than Todd and his buddies, who had perished when the ship went down.

In the silence the only sounds were the wind, the throbbing of the ship's engines, and the cry of seabirds. As I stood with my head bowed, I remembered another shipboard service that had taken place forty-eight years earlier, aboard the *Dorsetshire*. I imagined I could hear the plaintive strains of the German sailors' lament, "I had a comrade" as a flag-draped body disappeared into the sea.

June 13, 1989

There was no wild victory bash as we sailed for shore. People tended to gather in small groups, to celebrate

Before breaking up, the *Bismarck* team poses for a photo aboard the *Star Hercules* in June of 1989.

quietly or, like Todd and his buddies, with jokes and game after game of darts. But finding the *Bismarck* seemed bittersweet, tinged with sadness. The sadness was two-edged. Not only had we uncovered a war grave but our team was breaking up. Together we had lived through a great adventure. Now we were suddenly aware that our close-knit group was about to disappear.

As our ship neared port, I spent much of my spare time rehearsing the statement I planned to make to the German people about our discovery of the wreck. I wanted to assure them that I would respect the site as a war grave and that I recognized the fact that under international law the site still belonged to Germany. Hagen had translated the speech into German and now was coaching me on the correct pronunciation of the words. Meanwhile the thoughts of most of those on board turned to the future—to seeing friends and loved ones and eating a good meal and sleeping in one's own bed—thoughts not unlike those of the British sailors who'd caught the *Bismarck*, seen her sink, and then turned for home and a brief shore leave before sailing back to the cold gray battleground of the Atlantic.

Epilogue

After their rescue Franz, Heinz, Adi and Alois were sent to this prisoner-of-war camp in northern Ontario, Canada.

Most of the German sailors who survived the sinking of the *Bismarck* spent the rest of the war as prisoners. Once ashore they were taken to London for interrogation. This was the first battleship the British had sunk, and they were eager to know how big it was and how its gunnery and technical systems worked. But hard as they tried, they could get little information out of their captives. For example, although Alois Haberditz was an antiaircraft gunner, he told his interrogators he had worked solely as a cook. When they asked him how many people he fed, he answered that he didn't know—all he knew was there was always some soup in the pot when he had finished serving.

When the period of interrogation ended, the *Bismarck* survivors were sent to prisoner-of-war camps in various parts of Great Britain. Conditions were hard, and the food was terrible, so when the news came that they were being transferred to Canada, most were glad.

Along with hundreds of other captured Germans, they sailed to Halifax, Nova Scotia, and then were loaded onto trains. Franz Halke never forgot his first meal in Canada. Meat, vegetables and fresh eggs—the first fresh eggs he had seen since the *Bismarck*. Things were just as good when he and his comrades arrived at their prisoner-of-war camp in northern Ontario. There was as much food as they could eat, and they were allowed to build a soccer field and tennis courts. And the four friends—Franz Halke, Adi Eich, Heinz Jucknat and Alois Haberditz—were reunited. Lieutenant-Commander Müllenheim-Rechberg was sent to a camp for officers in southern Ontario. Franz, Heinz and Alois liked Canada so much that they returned there to live after the war.

The survivors of the *Bismarck* who are alive today vividly remember the experiences they went through in May 1941. Many of them still have nightmares, but they consider themselves lucky. As Alois Haberditz said to me, "I consider it to be my second birthday." Most of them still keep in touch with each other. Every few years they hold a reunion and get together to talk over old times. They have also become friends with many of the British sailors who took part in the battle.

More than two thousand young men died when the *Bismarck*

Surviving *Bismarck* sailors at a prisoner-of-war camp *(above)*. Nearly fifty years later, four *Bismarck* survivors look at video pictures of the wreck at the home of Baron von Müllenheim-Rechberg in Germany. The baron is on the far left.

sank, just one more example of the terrible human price of any war. The depth of this tragedy was brought home to me even more strongly when, a few weeks after our *Bismarck* expedition, my son Todd was killed in a car accident. Now I know the terrible sense of loss the parents of those young sailors must have felt when they heard that their sons had perished.

I will never get over Todd's death, but it has made me want to live the rest of my life as fully as I can. There is still much to be

Families and friends wave good-bye to the seamen of the *Bismarck* as the ship sails on its maiden voyage.

done in my field. The deep ocean is a vast unexplored storehouse of history. It is like a museum that has never been opened to the public. With the discovery of the *Bismarck* we have opened up a room in this museum, turned on the lights and invited in visitors. And this is only the beginning. In the coming years we will find other ships and open up other historical exhibits to public view.

And we will have an opportunity to relive the adventure and the tragedy of other great episodes in the history of the sea.

GLOSSARY

achtung: This is the German word for "attention."

aft: Near or at the back of a ship.

air intake shaft: A tube bringing fresh air to the lower parts of a ship.

altimeter: An instrument that lets *Argo's* pilots know how far their cameras are above objects on the ocean floor.

antiaircraft guns: Guns used on a ship for defense against enemy airplanes.

armament: The guns and equipment on a ship which are used for its defense.

bank: When an airplane flies in a curve with one wing higher than the other.

banquette: An upholstered bench built into a wall.

barrel: The metal tube of a gun. A 15-inch (38-centimetre) gun has a barrel whose opening is 15 inches (38 centimetres) across.

battle cruiser: A battle cruiser is lighter and faster than a battleship, but does not have as many guns.

bearing: The position of one ship in relation to the position of another.

biplane: An airplane with two sets of wings, usually one above the other.

boiler: A tank in which water is heated to produce steam.

bridge: The raised platform from which the captain or admiral directs a ship's course and issues the order to engage in battle.

bunker: The compartment on a ship used to store fuel.

collision mats: Mats used to cover holes in a ship caused by accidents or enemy shells.

conning tower: A metal-plated tower connected to the bridge from which the captain or admiral directs the ship when it is engaged in battle.

convoy: A group of ships carrying goods such as food and fuel which sail together under military escort.

debris: The pieces of wreckage from a ship, scattered over the ocean floor.

ensign: A banner or flag flown by a ship.

fantail: A fan-shaped overhang at the rear end of a ship.

fjord: A long, narrow arm of sea between high cliffs.

foray: A raid or brief invasion into enemy territory.

forward: Near or at the front of a ship.

Führer: The German word for "leader." This word was used mainly to refer to Adolf Hitler during the Nazi era.

galley: A ship's kitchen.

gun director: A periscope-like device that peeks above the roof of the control station through which the gunnery officer looks to determine where to aim the guns and when to fire.

gunmount: A support for a large gun.

heel: When a ship leans to one side.

hull: The frame or body of a ship without its superstructure.

hydrophone: An instrument for listening to sound transmitted through water.

infirmary: A ship's hospital.

interrogation: A close questioning in order to obtain information.

keel: The long metal ridge along the middle of a ship's bottom.

knot: The measure of a ship's speed equivalent to one nautical mile per hour.

magazine: The room on a ship where explosives are stored.

Nazi: A member of the political party controlling Germany from 1933-1945. The Nazi party was led by Adolf Hitler.

octopod: A sea-creature with eight arms.

port: The left-hand side of a ship when facing forward.

racist: A person who believes that one race is superior to another.

reconnaissance: The examination or survey of enemy territory to gain military information.

Reich: The German empire. The Nazi era (1933-1945) is often referred to as the Third Reich.

rudder: A broad, flat piece of metal hinged to the stern of a ship which is used for steering.

salvo: When two or more of a ship's guns fire at once.

sediment: Silt-like matter that settles on the ocean floor.

Sieg Heil: This German expression which means "To Victory" was used during the Nazi era as a greeting with a military salute.

shell: A metal case holding an explosive charge which is loaded into a big gun and fired.

sonar: A system used to detect and locate underwater objects by reflected sound waves.

starboard: The right-hand side of a ship when facing forward.

stern: The rear end of a ship.

swastika: A Nazi symbol shaped like a cross with four arms of equal length which bend at right angles in a clockwise direction.

swell: A heaving motion of the sea with waves that do not break.

three-stack cruiser: A battle cruiser with three smoke stacks.

torpedo: A cigar-shaped missile that travels underwater and explodes on impact.

transponder: A sonar device that receives a signal and then transmits its own signal. It is used as an underwater beacon to guide ships and vehicles.

turbine: An engine driven by a flow of steam.

turret: The low, flat, revolving tower which houses a ship's guns. The gunners operate the guns from inside the turret.

THE STORY OF THE *BISMARCK*

February 14, 1939
• Thousands of people cheer and give the Nazi salute to celebrate the launching of the *Bismarck*. The great ship slides down the slipway into the water for the first time.

May 19, 1941
• The *Bismarck* sets sail from Gotenhafen, occupied Poland, after months of preparations and sea trials. Her mission is to break out into the Atlantic and sink merchant ships bringing supplies to Great Britain.

May 21, 1941
• The pilot of a British Spitfire flying over the Norwegian fjords spots the *Bismarck* and *Prinz Eugen*. He photographs the German warships, proving to the British that the fearsome *Bismarck* is on the move.

May 24, 1941
• The British send the pride of their navy, the *Hood*, to stop the *Bismarck*. But in a battle which lasts only minutes, a shell from the *Bismarck* hits the *Hood*'s magazines and the British ship explodes.

May 26, 1941
• More than 24 hours after the *Bismarck* has shaken off the British ships chasing her, a pilot aboard a Catalina flying boat spots a dark shape "the size of a cigar box" in the water. It is the *Bismarck*.

May 26, 1941
• Later that night British Swordfish attack the *Bismarck*. One of the Swordfish fires a torpedo which jams the *Bismarck*'s rudders. The men on board can no longer steer their ship.

May 27, 1941
• As British ships close in on the wounded *Bismarck*, her huge guns continue to fire. Shells fall all around her creating splashes like tall fountains.

May 27, 1941
• An hour and a half after the first guns are fired, the *Bismarck*, full of shell holes and covered with flames, sinks beneath the waves. Hundreds of sailors find themselves in the cold waters of the Atlantic.

June 8, 1989
• Using *Argo*, an underwater robot with cameras, Robert Ballard and his team aboard the *Star Hercules* discover the wreck of the mighty *Bismarck* sitting upright on the ocean floor.

RECOMMENDED FURTHER READING

The Discovery of the Bismarck
by Robert D. Ballard 1990 (Warner Books Inc., U.S./Penguin Books, Canada/Hodder & Stoughton Publishers, U.K.)
An in-depth account of both the *Bismarck*'s final battle and her discovery by Robert Ballard with many pictures.

Exploring the Titanic
by Robert D. Ballard 1988 (Scholastic Inc., U.S./Pyramid, Octopus Books, U.K./Ashton Scholastic, Australia/Penguin Books, Canada)
The fascinating real-life adventure story of Robert Ballard's discovery of the *Titanic*.

Anne Frank: The Diary of a Young Girl Hiding From the Nazis
by Anne Frank 1990 (Doubleday, U.S.)
The actual journal of a 13-year-old girl in wartime Holland.

The Dolphin Crossing
by Jill Paton Walsh 1967 (Puffin Books, U.K. and Canada)
The gripping story of two boys who cross the English Channel to help British soldiers stranded in Dunkirk during World War II.

Great Battles of World War II
by John Macdonald 1986 (Macmillan Publishing Company, U.S./Michael Joseph Ltd., U.K.)
Major battles of the Second World War are described and fully illustrated.

PICTURE CREDITS

Front Cover: Painting by Ken Marschall (Bottom left) Joseph H. Bailey © National Geographic Society (Bottom middle) Painting by Ken Marschall (Bottom right) Quest Group
Front Flap: Bibliothek für Zeitgeschichte
Back Cover: (Top) *Sinking of the Bismarck* by Charles Turner, National Maritime Museum (Bottom) Painting by Ken Marschall
Back Flap: Joseph H. Bailey © National Geographic Society
Poster: (Top left) Painting by Claus Berger/Jörg Wischmann, Marineschule Murwik, *GEO* magazine (Bottom left) Imperial War Museum (Middle) Painting by Ken Marschall (Top right) Joseph H. Bailey © National Geographic Society (Bottom right) Quest Group
Endpapers: Alois Haberditz
Page 1: Bates Littlehales © National Geographic Society
2-3: *Battleship Bismarck* by Robert Taylor, courtesy of The Military Gallery
5: Joseph H. Bailey © National Geographic Society
6-7: Süddeutscher Verlag Bilderdienst
8-9: Painting by Ken Marschall
10: (Top left) Kirk Gustafson (Top middle) Billy Yunck (Top right) Joseph H. Bailey © National Geographic Society (Bottom) Joseph H. Bailey © National Geographic Society
11: Joseph H. Bailey © National Geographic Society
12: Bibliothek für Zeitgeschichte
13: Bundesarchiv
14: (Top left) Garzke & Dulin Collection (Bottom left) Ferdinand Urbahns (Right) Ferdinand Urbahns
14-15: Profile diagram by Ian Lawrence
15: Ferdinand Urbahns
16: (Left) Bundesarchiv (Left inset) Adolf Eich (Middle inset) Franz Halke (Right inset) Heinz Jucknat (Bottom) Profile diagram by Falcom Design Inc.
17: Bundesarchiv (Inset) Alois Haberditz
18: Zimmermann/Lindemann
19: Maps by Jack McMaster/Margo Stahl
20: Imperial War Museum
21: (Top) Burkard Baron von Müllenheim-Rechberg (Bottom) Painting by Wes Lowe

22: Map by Jack McMaster/Margo Stahl
23: Painting by Wes Lowe
24: (Top) Diagram by Jack McMaster/Margo Stahl (Top left) U.S. Naval Institute (Bottom) *The Destruction of H.M.S. Hood* by John Hamilton, Imperial War Museum
25: (Top) John Williams (Bottom) Diagram by Jack McMaster/Margo Stahl
26: (Top) Bundesarchiv (Bottom) Imperial War Museum
27: Painting by Wes Lowe
28-29: Painting by Wes Lowe
29: Diagram by Jack McMaster/Margo Stahl
30: Imperial War Museum
31: Ferdinand Urbahns
32: Imperial War Museum
32-33: Painting by Claus Berger/Jörg Wischmann, Marineschule Murwik, courtesy of *GEO* magazine
34: Imperial War Museum
35: Map and diagrams by Jack McMaster/Margo Stahl
36: Diagram by Jack McMaster/Margo Stahl
37: (Top) Bundesarchiv (Bottom) Burkard Baron von Müllenheim-Rechberg
38: Zimmermann/Lindemann
38-39: *Sinking of the Bismarck* by Charles Turner, National Maritime Museum
40: Imperial War Museum
41: Popperfoto
42: Joseph H. Bailey © National Geographic Society
43: (Top) Marie Tharp, Oceanographic Cartographer (Bottom) Joseph H. Bailey © National Geographic Society
44: Diagram by Jack McMaster/Margo Stahl (Bottom) Todd Ballard
45: Joseph H. Bailey © National Geographic Society
46: Joseph H. Bailey © National Geographic Society
47: (Top) Joseph H. Bailey © National Geographic Society (Bottom) George Mobley © National Geographic Society
48: (Inset) Joseph H. Bailey © National Geographic Society (Left) Diagram by Jack McMaster/Margo Stahl

49: Joseph H. Bailey © National Geographic Society
50: Joseph H. Bailey © National Geographic Society
51: Painting by Ken Marschall
52: (Top) Painting by Ken Marschall (Bottom) Bundesarchiv
52-53: Painting by Ken Marschall
54: (Top left) Quest Group (Middle left) Bundesarchiv (Bottom left) Zimmermann/Lindemann (Top right) Quest Group (Bottom right) Painting by Ken Marschall
55: (Top) Painting by Ken Marschall (Bottom) Bundesarchiv
56: (Top) Bundesarchiv (Bottom) Quest Group
57: (Top left) Painting by Ken Marschall (Middle left) Zimmermann/Lindemann (Bottom left) Quest Group (Right) Diagram by Wes Lowe
58: (Top) Joseph H. Bailey © National Geographic Society (Bottom) Quest Group
59: Joseph H. Bailey © National Geographic Society
60: Franz Halke
61: (Top) Imperial War Museum (Middle) Joseph H. Bailey © National Geographic Society (Bottom) Otto Höntzsch
63: Diagrams by Jack McMaster

Madison Press Books would like to thank the following people for their assistance and advice:
Adolf Eich, Alois Haberditz, Franz Halke, Heinz Jucknat and Burkard Baron von Müllenheim-Rechberg, survivors of the *Bismarck*; Kirk Gustafson and Billy Yunck; John Siswick; Barbara Earle of Odyssey Corporation; Bill Allen, Lisa Page, Chris Weber and Peter Schnall of the National Geographic Society; Gretchen McManamin of the Woods Hole Oceanographic Institution; and Bill Garzke and Bob Dulin.